COMPUTER HOT KEY MASTERY

OPERATE THE COMPUTER SEAMLESSLY & EFFICIENTLY

MOMOH S.O

CONTENTS

PREFACE

In a world where the use of computer has become a common place and also the increasing work from home and remote mindset,increasing adoption of free-lancing andremote work for hire & gig economy.

Hence the need to address efficiency and ease of use of computers and PCs as they are used mainly for these works and operations.

This book lists some hot keys or keyboard

shortcuts that facilitate and make the operation of the computer seamless.

ABOUT THE AUTHOR

MOMOH S.O is a Programmer,
Web developer,system
analyst,graphic designer,a
writer with years of experience
in practice and the
use of the computer.He
has an M.sc in computer
engineering and technology
and is proficient in
programming languages such

as python,javascript,php,html as well as CSS and Jquery.

TABLE OF CONTENT

SUMMARY

In a world of increasing digitization, technological inclination & dependence,working remotely, **work from home,online interactions** and social media explosion,online marketing etc. **The use of computer has become the order of the day from home , offices, businesses, companies to the corporate world.**

Hence the need for the mastery of computer keyboards and other operations around the computer.
This book contains various keyboard key combinations and their functions to facilitate a seamless and easy operation of the computer,Increase efficiency and maximize output.

INTRODUCTION

This book **Computer hot key mastery** serves as a guide,manual, & practice and reference material and gives a rock solid start to the use of the computer keyboard and operations around the computer.

With a mastery of the use of the computer hotkeys,one can Seamlessly navigate computer operations hitch-free without a glitch and work

productively,efficiently
turn scale up output.

 From the use of typing,editing,
 proofreading software
and apps such as;word
document(docx),
 power
point(pptx),spreadsheet(xlsx).
 Graphic design apps
and tools like;
 Adobe photo -
shop,paint,website
 development and architectural
 and coding tools such
as translators,
 IDEs,text editors,core

draw,graph pads
and other analytical tools and
gaming tools & video games all
require the use of computer
 hotkeys.

COMMON HOTKEYS
ANDSHORTCUTS

HOT KEYS ARE KEYS OR A

combination of hot keys or keyboard shortcut keys. From control(CTRL) plus C to carry out COPY operation or copy a highlighted item or object,to more complex or advanced operations involving the combination of multiple keys such taking screenshot of a computer screen and so on.As we will see in subsequent pages.

Control(Ctrl) & C

This hotkey combination executes COPY function. When pressed or combined on a highlighted item,object(s), or list(s) or page,it is copied to the clipboard and ready to be pasted or transferred.

USE

To use,simply hold the Ctrl button & then press letter C.The item(s) is copied instantly.

Control(Ctrl) & v

This is for Paste function. Long press the Ctrl button & press V This pastes the content of the Clipboard or copied item in to a folder or a page.

Control(Ctrl) & X

This cuts or deletes a highlighted item or element(s).

Shift(↑) & delete
This deletes an object or item permanently and not moved to the recycle bin.

Control(Ctrl) & A
This selects or highlights all items in a given window or folder or page.

Alt & F4 key
To a window or an open program

Also to display the shutdown dialogue box.

Alt & tab key

To move between open task bar programs or open apps.

Ctrl & Alt & tab key

To switch between opened tabs or items.

Windows key & tab
To flip through open items Or tabs

Ctrl & window key & tab then

arrow(direction key)

To cycle through opened program using arrow keys

Alt & esc

Move through items in order.

Alt & arrow up

Open folder upwards

Windows logo & E

Opens the window

explorer or computer.

Windows logo & F
Deep Searches through the
entire computer

Control (Ctrl) & Z
Undo an
action,settings or
a command.

Control(ctrl) & Y
Redo an action or

command that
was modified.

Windows key & M
Minimizes the entire windows
Opened

Windows key & L
Locks the PC screen

Windows key & up arrow
Restores minimized windows

Control(ctrl) & shift& tab
Move in reverse through tabs

Windows key & D
Shows the desktop

home screen

Windows key & space bar
To peek at the desktop view

COMPUTER KEYBOARD

HOTKEYS & SHORTCUT KEYS

WINDOWS & X

To open wireless,volume,battery... control points.

Shift(↑) & tab
Go back up page slowly

Control & tab
Sift through opened tabs or next tabs in opened ordered.

CONTROL(CTRL) & ALT & arrow key{L-R-U-D)
Rotates the entire screen or window left,right,up & down.

Windows key & Numbers
Opens task bar programs in order of positioning on task bar.

Windows key & Home
Leaves only the open window active and others minimized.

Control(ctrl) & E
Opens the computer

or launcher

**Control(ctrl) &
Shift(↑) & prt sc**
**To grab a screen or
screenshot the monitor**

**Web Applications
browser Hot keys
(OPERA MINI,UC
WEBROWSER,FIRE FOX
& CHROME APPS)**

The web browser applications are commonly used for online browsing and surfing the internet.Hence the need to familiarize with the ease of access or accessibility hot keys and navigating through tabs, managing tabs, and multi-tasking with the web app. Some of these hot keys and combination helps ease operations and lessen the use of mouse to go through the web page.

Control & O

To open open files
or folders on
the computer.

Control C

To copy a selected
or highlighted
item on the screen.

Control & V

To paste a copied

file,words,pages or
items on the clipboard.

Control & F

To search for an item
on the browser
or open page.

Control & numbers(1-9 etc)

Move through
opened tabs in a
serial order or orders
they are open.
Say tab1,tab2...

Control & P

**Prints a document
or produce
a pdf file of a web page.
Initiates printing
of a web page
through a printer.**

Control & A

**Highlights the entire web page
for copying.**

Control & W

**Closes an open
window or tab**

Alt & arrow keys(L & R)
Moves between opened tabs
from left to right

Control(ctrl) & H
Gives or displays
the history.

Control(ctrl) & +
Zooms in to the web
page-enlarges

Control(ctrl) & -
Zooms out in to the

**page- shrinks
page.**

Control(ctrl) & R
**Reloads or refreshes
a web page**

VLC AND OTHER VIDEO OR
Media player Hotkeys

Control(ctrl) & Up arrow
Increases or raises
the volume up

Control(ctrl) & down arrow
Decreases the volume

Control(ctrl) & right arrow
Forward or fast
forwards the video
or song.

Control(ctrl) & left arrow
Rewinds or takes
back the video.

Letter N
Moves to the Next the video

Letter P
Moves to the previous video

ESC(escape) key
Removes full-screen mode

Space bar
Pauses or plays a video or song

Word docs,Spreadsheet & power point,paint,text editor,journal,Notepads,etc.Hot keys

Control & O

To open open files
or folders on
the computer.

Control C

To copy a selected or highlighted item on the screen.

Control & V

To paste a copied file,words,pages or items on the clipboard.

CONTROL & F

To find an item

CONTROL (CTRL) & Z

To undo a change to a document or action,returning it back to it's original form.

Control(ctrl) & N

Open or start a new documents or opens a blank page or new page.

Control(ctrl) & S

Save page or save changes

Control(ctrl) & P

Print page or document

Control(ctrl) & Y
Redo a previous/ recent action

Control(ctrl) & X
Cut or remove a selection

Control(ctrl) & B
Make a text or selection bold

Control(ctrl) & I
Make selection appear in italics form.

Control(ctrl) & U

Underlines a text or selection

Control(ctrl) & J
Justify selection and align

Control(ctrl) & L
Align text or selection to the left

Control(ctrl) & R
Aligns text or selection to the right

Control(ctrl)

& Shift( ) & >

Increases or enlarges a text or selection

Control(ctrl) & 1

This leaves a single blank line below a line of text.

Control(ctrl) & Shift( ) & <

Decreases a text or selection size

Control(ctrl) & Up arrow

Moves cursor upwards or towards previous lines.

Control(ctrl) & down arrow
Moves cursor downwards or towards lower lines or page.

Control(ctrl) & left arrow
Moves cursor to the left

Control(ctrl) &

right arrow

Moves the cursor

to the right
side of the page.

Control(ctrl) & Home
Takes you to the

beginning of
the document.

Control (ctrl) & delete
Delete subsequent word

Control(ctrl) & end
Takes you to the
beginning of
the document.

Control(ctrl) & L
Move selected texts to the left
or left alignment.

Control(ctrl) & R
Move selected texts

to the right
or right alignment.

Control(ctrl) & E
Move selected texts
to the middle

or middle alignment.

CONCLUSION

Computer hot keys
are essential and near
compulsory if we ever
want to be efficient and
move speedily &
efficiently working with
PCs and our
computers.In a fast
advancing digital world
where the use of computers
have become a
common place and
order of the day.
From free-lancing,
online gigs,

such as proof-reading & editing, coding,graphic design,video editing,scripting,web design,spreadsheet & other documents to use in the corporate world with increasing remoteness and so on.

This book 'Computer hot key Mastery ' facilitates a smooth learning curve.

*Begin your journey
to computer
Mastery seamlessly!*

**Please leave a Rating in
the Amazon store.**

www.ingramcontent.com/pod-product-compliance
Lightning Source LLC
LaVergne TN
LVHW072052060326
832903LV00054B/403